Washington Stories

By Carol M. Elliott

Contents

Setting the Stage

Teacher Read Aloud	2
Vocabulary	3
Fluency Warm-Up	4
Comprehension Warm-Up	5

Act I
Reader's Theater:

Dolley Madison Saves George!	6–11

Intermission 12

Act II
Connected Readings:

In 1880	13
In 1932	14
In 1983	15

Curtain Call 16

Setting the Stage
Teacher Read Aloud

The White House, located in Washington, D.C., is the official home and office of the President of the United States. All of the American Presidents except George Washington have lived in the White House.

The history of the White House started in 1792. A contest was held to see who could come up with the best design. James Hoban won the design contest and a $500 prize. President George Washington helped choose the building site. The actual building began in 1792. John Adams, the second President, was the first to move into the White House in 1800.

The White House was burned during the War of 1812, during the presidency of James Madison. Hoban worked on the reconstruction of the White House. By 1817, the White House was ready for then President James Monroe.

There are 132 rooms and 35 bathrooms in the White House. It also has a swimming pool, movie theater, bowling lane, basketball court, and a jogging track.

The White House is a symbol of America, its government, and the American people. This historic site in Washington, D.C., attracts more than 1.5 million visitors every year.

In Acts I and II of this book, you will read stories about life in Washington, D.C., in 1814, in 1880, in 1932, and in 1983. You will also practice your reading. Use the vocabulary and warm-ups on the next three pages to get ready.

The White House, 1814

John Adams

VOCABULARY THINK TANK

If a home was burning, how would the people replace the things lost in the fire?

Vocabulary

Read and review these words with a partner. This will help prepare you for reading the stories in this book.

Burning—destroying with fire

Cannon—a large gun that shoots cannon balls

Replace—to take the place of something lost

Shame—a painful, embarrassing feeling

Soldiers—people who fight in an army

Trunk—a large case for holding clothes and other things

Fluency Warm-Up:
Using Expression

Fluent readers read with **expression**. Expression means to have feeling in your voice. Try to show how your character is feeling — happy or sad or mad!

What clues are in the text that help you understand feelings? Maybe you see an exclamation point or all capital letters. Or maybe you just have to use your imagination. Then change your voice to express loud or soft feelings.

FLUENCY PRACTICE

Read these sentences three times. Sound happy the first time, sad the second time, and mad the third time.

1. She gave me a slice of bread.
2. Look at that.
3. That is mine.

Comprehension Warm-Up:
Asking Questions

It is a good idea to **ask questions** before, during, and after you read. Asking questions will help you think more about the story and understand it better.

Make sure you don't just read words. You need to be thinking about what you are reading. Think about what is happening and what might happen next. Ask yourself what the author is trying to teach you or tell you.

COMPREHENSION TIP

As you read, ask yourself questions like these. Think about the answers.

- What does this sentence mean?
- Why is this character acting this way?
- What am I supposed to learn from this?

ACT 1 READER'S THEATER

Dolley Madison Saves George!

CAST OF CHARACTERS FOR 6 PLAYERS

Narrator	French John
President Madison	British soldier 1
Dolley Madison	British soldier 2

Narrator: It is Monday morning, August 22nd, 1814. The British Army is advancing toward Washington, D.C. The United States Army is preparing for battle. President James Madison and First Lady Dolley Madison are deciding what to do.

Pres. Madison: I need to join the general. I have to help plan this battle. But I worry about leaving you here alone.

Dolley Madison: Do not worry about me. I will be fine. Besides I am not alone. The servants are here.

Pres. Madison: Are you sure you want to stay? Many people are leaving the city. You could go too.

Dolley Madison: I want to stay here at the White House. It is our home. I am not afraid. I believe that you and the Army will beat the British. And when you return, we will have a wonderful dinner for you and the officers.

Pres. Madison: I will try to return in two to three days. Please take care of yourself, my dear.

Narrator: The next day President Madison sent a message to his wife.

French John: This message just came. It is from the President.

Dolley Madison (reading): It says the enemy seems stronger than had been reported. He wants us to be ready to leave. He is afraid if the British do get through, they will destroy the city.

French John: What do you want us to do? Should we prepare to leave? Or should we prepare to fight? I could put a **cannon** at the gate!

Dolley Madison: I suppose we must get ready to leave, but I am not leaving yet. I still believe our Army will win and we will have a party tomorrow night.

FLUENCY TIP

How is French John feeling? Change your voice to show his feelings as he asks Dolley Madison what to do.

French John: I hope you're right. But I heard that the **soldiers** who were supposed to guard the city have left.

Narrator: Dolley and the servants packed several **trunks**. Then Dolley sat down to write a letter to her sister.

Dolley Madison (*writing*): I have packed the President's important papers in trunks. Our things must be left behind as there aren't enough wagons to move everything. Our friends are all gone. I am not leaving, though. I want to wait for Mr. Madison.

Narrator: The next day was Wednesday, August 24th. Dolley Madison had the table set for 40 people. She had the servants prepare a dinner. She still hoped that the U.S. Army would win. Then she continued her letter to her sister.

DOLLEY MADISON *(writing)*: Since sunrise, I have used my spyglass to look for my dear husband and his friends. But they do not come. There has been a battle in a town a few miles from here. I can hear the sound of the cannon!

FRENCH JOHN: Two messengers are here covered with dust. They say we are to leave—now! The enemy is almost here!

DOLLEY MADISON: I will not leave without the large painting of General Washington. He is the father of our country, and the picture must be saved.

FRENCH JOHN: But that picture is fixed to the wall. We can't take the time to undo that.

DOLLEY MADISON: Then break the frame! I will not leave without the painting!

NARRATOR: Finally, Dolley Madison and the servants left the White House. They had saved the picture of George Washington. The British soldiers arrived a few hours later. The table was still set.

FLUENCY TIP

How is Dolley Madison feeling? Use loudness in your voice to express her strong feelings.

British soldier 1: So this is their President's palace.

British soldier 2: And look here. They must have been planning a party.

British soldier 1: It would be a **shame** to waste all this food. Let's eat!

Narrator: After the soldiers had eaten, they took a look around the White House.

British soldier 1: This White House isn't so special. Look at this broken frame hanging here on the wall.

British soldier 2: Yes, we will be doing them a favor by **burning** this place down!

Narrator: The enemy soldiers laughed as they set fire to the White House. Then they set fire to many other buildings. Soon the city was burning. Three days later, the Madisons returned to their home.

Dolley Madison: What a shame! Our lovely home is gone!

Pres. Madison: Oh, Dolley, I am sorry that the army could not stop them.

Dolley Madison: The most important thing, my dear husband, is that you are safe. We will rebuild the White House. The British will not win.

Pres. Madison: I suppose we can **replace** most of what was lost. Thank you for saving my important papers. Ah, but the picture of George Washington! How will we ever replace that?

Dolley Madison: We will only need to replace the frame. We had to break it to remove the painting, but the picture was saved!

Pres. Madison: That's great! What a wonderful and brave woman you are!

FLUENCY TIP
President Madison's feelings change on this page. Express this change from sad to proud in your reading.

INTERMISSION

Self-Check

Did you read with expression?

Comprehension Prompters

1. Why did Dolley feel she needed to save the painting of George Washington?
2. What would you ask the author if you could talk to her?
3. Why do you think the British wanted to burn the White House?

Actor's Corner

What would you have done if you were Dolley Madison and the British were coming? With a partner, talk about what you would have done.
- How long would you have stayed in the White House?
- What would you have tried to save?

ACT II CONNECTED READINGS

In 1880

In 1880 Helen moved to Washington, D.C. She met Marvin. He showed her around.

They walked several blocks. Then Marvin said, "That is the White House. The President lives there. And way over there is the Capitol."

The open land between the White House and the Capitol was swampy. They saw a strange thing.

"That will be a monument to George Washington. But it's not done," Marvin said.

"Was he the one who freed the slaves?" asked Helen.

"No, that was Lincoln. There's no monument to him," said Marvin.

"That's a **shame**. There should be one," said Helen.

FLUENCY TIP

Reread Helen's last line. Read it with confidence and strength in your voice.

In 1932

In the 1930s, many people were poor. They wrote to First Lady Mrs. Roosevelt asking for help. Many who wrote were children.

January 1932

Dear Mrs. Roosevelt

Our father is out of work. He had worked for the railroad for 15 years. Could you help him get a job? He wants to work, but says these are hard times.

I am 9 years old. I do not have a coat. I can't go to school without a coat. My brother needs glasses and a coat.

We read in the papers how good you are to the poor. We thought maybe you could help us. Could you please send just a small trunk of items? We would be thankful all of our lives.

Susan and Jim Johnson

FLUENCY TIP

Read the letter as if the children were saying the words. Use loudness and softness to express their feelings.

In 1983

In April 1983, Mr. Green's third grade class went to Washington, D.C. In the White House, they saw a large painting of George Washington.

Rosa asked, "Is that the painting Dolley Madison saved?"

"Yes," replied the guide. "I'm glad you know that story. We need to remember the brave."

The class saw museums, the Capitol, the Washington Monument, and the Lincoln Memorial. Then they went to see the new Vietnam Veterans Memorial.

The black wall listed the names of Americans who had died in the war. A man was leaning on the wall and crying quietly. His finger traced a **soldier's** name.

Rosa whispered, "We need to remember the brave."

FLUENCY TIP

Notice that Rosa "whispered." Make sure you whisper when you read that line.

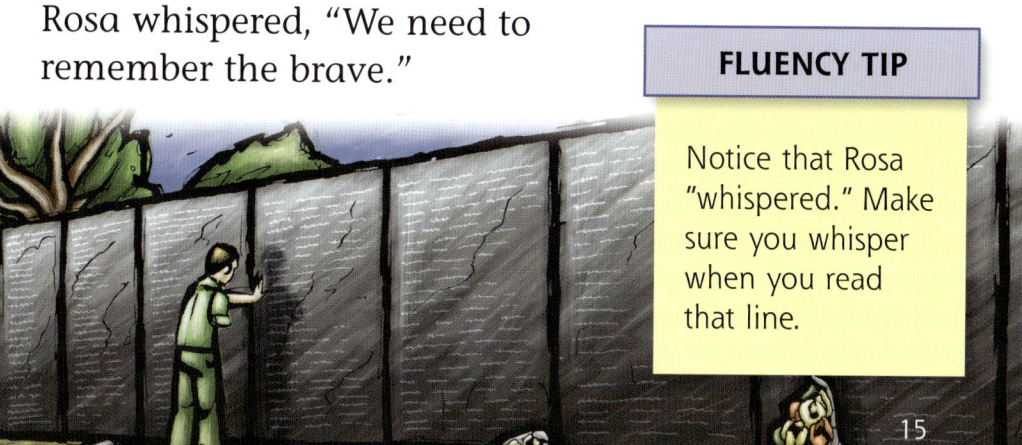

CURTAIN CALL

Reread

Go back and reread your assigned Act II story several more times aloud. Remember to use expression. The more you practice, the better reader you will become!

Comprehension Prompters

1. "In 1880": Write at least two questions about Washington, D.C., during this time.
2. "In 1932": Why are the children writing to the President's wife?
3. "In 1983": This story refers to "the brave" twice. Who are "the brave"?

Taking It Further

With a partner, do some research on Washington, D.C., and write a story about it. Then read your story aloud to the class. Choose a topic below.
- Write a story about one of the famous people or buildings in the city.
- Write a story about what it would be like, or is like, to live in D.C.